T0266736

How to Travel

—

Contents

1. How to Choose a Destination 7
2. What Is 'Exotic'? 12
3. The Suspicion of Happiness 14
4. Anxiety 16
5. Small Pleasures 18
6. Water Towers 25
7. The Importance of the Sun 27
8. Travel as a Cure for Shyness 30
9. The Pleasure of the Airport 36
10. The Pleasure of the Flight 39
11. Pretty Cities 41
12. The Pleasure of Otherness 44
13. The Longing to Talk to Strangers 46
14. The Vulnerability of Perfection to Emotional Troubles 48
15. The Importance of Family Holidays 51
16. The Pleasure of the Romantic Minibreak 53
17. The Little Restaurant 55
18. In Defence of Crowds 58
19. The Pleasure of Room Service 63
20. The Pleasures of Nature 64
21. Drawing Rather than Taking Photographs 66
22. Holiday Fling 78
23. Travelling for Perspective 80
24. Travel and Pilgrimages 85
25. How to Spend a Few Days in Paris 89
26. How to Come Home 102
27. The Advantages of Staying at Home 104
28. Cherishing Memories 107
29. The Shortest Trip: Going for a Walk 109
30. The Shortest Travel Quiz 116

One of the greatest conundrums
of travel also happens
to have the most basic ring to it:
where should we go?

1.
How to Choose a Destination

Our societies are not shy about presenting us with options, of course, but they are also content to leave us alone with the many deeper complexities beneath the business of choosing.

A satisfying answer is less simple than it seems, for it requires us to have a deep understanding of ourselves, a good grasp of the nature of the world and an implicit philosophy of happiness.

Every destination has a character: that is, it emphasises and promotes a particular aspect of human nature. Some, like the long, empty beaches of South Australia, invite us to serenity; others, like the suburbs of Amsterdam, reinforce the pleasures of bourgeois sobriety. Los Angeles speaks to our dormant worldly ambitions and foregrounds a less squeamish attitude to money; Miami or Rio de Janeiro can loosen inhibition and reserve and tug us towards a relaxed sensuality.

The destination we find ourselves drawn to reflects an underlying sense of what is currently missing or under-supported in our lives. We are seeking, through our travels, not just to see new places, but also to become fuller, more complete beings. The destination promises to correct imbalances in our psyches, for we are all inevitably a little lacking or excessive in one area or another. The place we go to should, ideally, help to teach us certain lessons that we know we need to hear. Our destinations are a guide to, and a goad for, who we are trying to become.

To make a wise choice about where to travel, therefore, we should look first not so much at the outer world but at the inner one. We need to ask ourselves what is missing or presently too weak within us, and on that basis, set about identifying a location somewhere on the planet – in the wilderness or a city, in the tropics or by a glacier – with the power to help us develop into the sort of people we need to become.

Travel accedes to its true nobility when we ensure that the physical journey can support a well-defined inner journey towards maturity and emotional health.

Where would you like to go?

9

2.
What Is 'Exotic'?

Our societies have a strong sense of what makes a destination 'exotic'. Normally, the word is associated with palm trees, temples to unfamiliar gods, humid heat and unknown animals.

But, stripped to its essence, 'exotic' has nothing to do with the prescriptive list of places with which it is typically associated. It merely means anywhere we yearn to go which we suspect has something important to teach us. Each of us is likely to have a private atlas of destinations that sound exotic to our ears, and which we need the courage and patience to unearth and bring into focus. The exotic is evidence of what is missing in ourselves.

We might be inspired to follow our own definitions of exoticism by the example of the nineteenth-century politician and writer Benjamin Disraeli. In one of his novels, *Coningsby,* the central character – a thinly disguised version of the author – develops a fascination for the factories and heavy industry of northern England. Though he and his friends have been used to holidaying in the countryside, the narrator admits that what would be truly exotic for him would be to go and spend two weeks investigating steel mills, cotton factories and coal mines. He does so, and the experience transforms him into a more serious and resolute person.

The modern equivalent would be someone cancelling a break in southern Spain to take a life-expanding trip to the appliance factories of the Ruhr valley or the data-storage centres of Montana.

Sadly, too often, we're shy about investigating what might really be exotic to us. We may end up in more clichéd 'exotic' places from a shyness about locating and declaring our true interests. We're often still at the dawn of properly knowing ourselves. At least we can be assured that no one will mock or say we're weird if we reveal we're off to Phuket or Barbados. But what is properly exotic to us might lie somewhere quite different, in the suburbs of Yokohama, a hilltop retreat in Bavaria or the Norwegian hamlet of Sveagruva.

We should dare to ask ourselves what feels properly exotic to us – even if it has no palm tree anywhere in the vicinity and occupies no space in any brochure – and ensure we have the resolve to pay proper homage to it in our next itinerary.

3.
The Suspicion of Happiness

Enjoying life is, in theory, deeply desirable, but we'd be wise to note how challenging it can be in reality – a fact with which our travels tend to confront us starkly. Suddenly, for a little while, by the pool or in the mountains, we may have nothing to do other than to be happy. The prospect can be truly alarming.

We tend to have three big fears:

i)	ii)	iii)
If I settle back, throw away my cares for a time and enjoy what I have, I will lose the will to strive – which has been responsible for everything I have achieved to date.	Enjoying beauty and comfort is selfish. There is, after all, simply so much suffering around.	Enjoying life is not serious.

In Aesop's famous fable, 'The Grasshopper and the Ant', all summer long, the ant labours away and when winter comes, she has enough food to survive. All summer long, the grasshopper enjoys herself – and is starving the next winter. The moral of the story is likely to have burnt itself into our consciousness from a young age. Relaxation can be dangerous.

But none of our three fears stand up to closer examination:

i)	ii)	iii)
We can retain a sure hold on our striving-inducing dissatisfactions and, at the same time, occasionally savour the fragile harmony and beauty of a moment. In any case, unless we learn how to appreciate what we have, there is no point striving for more. Further gains are only worthwhile if our appreciative capacities are already functioning properly.	Appreciation does not rule out compassion. Indeed, the more satisfied and rested we are, the more strength we have to bring to bear on the troubles of others. Being personally happy generates the best possible basis for helping to alleviate the griefs of strangers and friends.	We don't have to enjoy life the way the adverts tell us: we can carve out our own vision of pleasure, every bit as serious and dignified as we wish it to be.

We should go easy on ourselves for needing a little encouragement to accept a very unfamiliar situation: a few moments of happiness.

4.
Anxiety

A huge motive for travelling is the search for calm. But we should be modest about how calm we can ever be. We are, after all, human beings – creatures for whom serenity is not a native state.

A degree of anxiety is fundamental to our nature for well-founded reasons:

• Because we are intensely vulnerable physical beings, a complicated network of fragile organs deeply affected by the vagaries of our outer and inner worlds.

• Because we can imagine so much more than we can ever have and live in mobile-driven, mediatised societies where envy and restlessness are constants.

• Because we are the descendants of the great worriers of the species (the others having been trampled and torn apart by wild animals) and because we still carry in our bones – into the calm of the jasmine-scented holiday resort – the terrors of the savannah.

• Because we rely for our self-esteem and sense of comfort on the love of people we cannot control and whose needs and hopes will never align seamlessly with our own.

We should gently laugh at the challenges of relaxation. There is no need – on top of everything else – to be anxious that we are anxious. The mood is no sign that our lives have gone wrong, merely that we are alive.

We should be more careful when heading for destinations that we imagine will spare us every anxiety. We can go, but with a little more scepticism about our likely mood. It is rare to be uncomplicatedly happy for longer than fifteen minutes.

5.
Small Pleasures

To generalise, our age believes in Big Pleasures. We've inherited a romantic suspicion of the ordinary (which is taken to be mediocre, dull and uninspiring) and work with a corresponding assumption that things that are unique, hard to find or deeply unfamiliar are naturally fitted to delight us more. We subtly like high prices. If something is cheap or free, it's a little harder to appreciate.

The approach isn't wholly wrong, but unwittingly it exhibits a vicious and unhelpful bias against the cheap, the easily available, the ordinary and the small-scale.

Yet the paradoxical aspect of pleasure is how promiscuous it can prove to be. It doesn't neatly collect in expensive boutiques. It can refuse to stick with us in the big museum. It is remarkably vulnerable to emotional trouble, sulks and casual bad moods.

Travels are often filled with small pleasures. Perhaps it was the rye bread on the terrace of the hotel, the field of dandelions near the canal, a conversation with someone washing clothes at a fountain, the sound of the city heard on a walk through the park at night...

Such things can lack prestige or social support. They sound rather minor. They wouldn't be what one would ordinarily pick out as highlights of a journey.

Yet a pleasure may look very minor – eating a fig, saying a word in a new language, browsing in a spice shop – and yet be anything but. If properly grasped and elaborated upon, these sorts of activities may be among the most moving and satisfying we can ever hope to have.

Travels are often filled with small pleasures
…the field of dandelions near the canal.

A pleasure may look very minor...
and yet be anything but.

The smallness of a pleasure isn't really an assessment of how much it has to offer us: it is a reflection of how many good things the world unfairly neglects. We should dare to fully savour the modest pleasures offered to us by our trips.

Bernd and Hilla Becher,
*Water Towers,*1972–2009

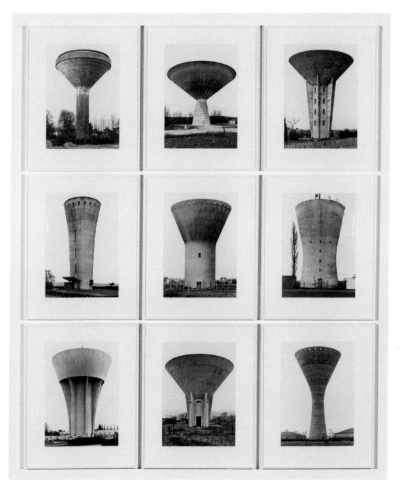

6.
Water Towers

Our societies are constantly sending out signals about what is potentially fascinating, impressive or beautiful to visit. They have been very good at getting us to see the charms of dolphins, mountains, little villages in rural France and art deco hotels from the 1920s. These are all very worthy objects of delight, but the list could be so much wider.

In 1972, a German couple – Bernd and Hilla Becher – started to photograph water towers across Germany and the United States. These industrial structures were amongst the least admired of all buildings; they were deemed hulking and brutish and people would get predictably furious if ever one was planned near where they lived.

Yet the Bechers' photographs – arranged in serene and elegant frames, and hung in sequences along gallery walls – showed just how beautiful these towers actually were. One could appreciate their patterns of rust and their rugged authenticity; their legs had a distinct dignity and playfulness. They were like curious monuments in the landscape.

The real point of the Bechers' exercise wasn't specifically about water-storage facilities. The towers provided an example for a much wider point: that there is a great deal more that is lovely and interesting in the world than we have yet been encouraged to suspect.

The example of these photographs teaches us something else. To gain access to the full range of what is valuable, we need to suspect that the current list of what is worth seeing is radically incomplete – and we should be ready to start expanding it by ourselves, one tower at a time.

7.
The Importance of the Sun

We're supposed to be serious people with important things on our minds. But we can admit it without guilt: seeking sun is one of the central, and most important, motives behind going travelling.

We have, after all, been cold for so long. For months, we have been fending off wind, rain and despair. Through the impossibly long winter and freezing spring, we have been swaddling ourselves in layers. We hardly ever see our own legs – beyond a reluctant glance at their pallor in the bath. We have eaten for comfort. And it shows, a bit. But deep within us, we know we are essentially made for sunny mornings, hot lazy afternoons and warm nights that echo to the sound of cicadas.

On the beach, there are recliners under big straw sunshades. The water is warm. The heat envelops us and warms us to the core. Every day, the sky is perfectly blue and unclouded. From the hotel balcony, we can look out onto a succession of arid and scrubby hills; we love the sight of the baked and cracked earth because it speaks of weeks upon weeks of hot, dry weather.

It can suddenly seem inhuman that our species has so cleverly managed to sustain itself in places that are windswept, wet and dreary for almost the whole year. We have made good lives for ourselves up there – in Wiesbaden, Trondheim, Hyvinkää and Calgary. But at such a cost.

Sunshine isn't merely 'nice'. It has a profound role in our lives. It is an agent of moral qualities: generosity, courage, the appreciation of the present moment and a confidence in our surroundings. We can feel our character changing in the sun: becoming something we like a lot more. When the world seems bountiful and easy (as it does in the heat), material accumulation looks less impressive or necessary. When we can have so much pleasure from sitting in a T-shirt and shorts and feasting on a feta and tomato salad, competing wildly for promotion loses its point. When it is so hot, there is no point even trying to read – or think too much.

The sun can correct our usual vices. The ways of the north are liable to be overly dominant and entrenched in our lives. We need to lie on the beach not because we are light-minded or indolent, but because we can be so dangerously dutiful, serious, hard-working, disconnected from our body, over-cerebral and cautious.

It is a deeply noble search for wisdom and balance (which are the ideal goals of art, civilisation and travel) that has led us here – to an enchanting world of sun cream, dark glasses, recliners and vividly coloured cocktails by the pool.

8.
Travel as a Cure for Shyness

On the first day in Japan, it was truly difficult. You went into the corner shop just off the main Motomachi shopping street to buy a prepaid mobile card. You pointed at your phone, said 'Hello, it's me', and mimed the actions of someone making a call. But it was useless. Mr Nishimura couldn't understand you at all. You were hot and flustered (it was 30°C and pretty humid) and felt very young again and an unusually big idiot.

It evoked the time at school when you were supposed to make a speech and your mind went blank, and the painful evenings at college when everybody else seemed to be heading off somewhere and you weren't sure if you could ask to join in.

Over the years, in your life back home, you have learned how to avoid situations of awkwardness. You have become an expert at working around your diffidence and your fear of being the unwelcome focus of attention. But, of course, there's been a price to pay for your expertise at defensiveness. Whenever something feels alien or in any way threatening, your instinct has been to retreat, and you've missed out on a lot.

But now, in Japan, fitting in is no longer an option. You are the stupid foreigner. Of course you can't know what you are supposed to do. Everyone stares at you wherever you go.

It sounds bad but, surprisingly, such extremity starts to offer you a certain sort of liberation. Maybe fitting in is overrated. Maybe not looking like a fool is simply not an option in any rich and interesting life, wherever it may unfold.

So you steel your nerves. You go back to the shop. You buy some wasabi-flavoured crisps and give the guy at the till a big smile. He grins back. You're learning. You opt to rent an apartment near the elegant Sankeien Gardens from a really nice guy called Kazutaka. A few days after, you drop in on the shop again and buy a packet of Chokobi mini star-shaped chocolate biscuits (they look fun). You make a joke about the rain. You say 'ame desu' – which you'd practised after breakfast and hopefully means something like 'it's raining' – and gesture drolly at your wet hair. Mr Nishimura beams at you.

Through travel, you're freeing yourself from your inhibitions. You're growing up – and into yourself. Our journeys can teach us a vital skill: that of not minding so much if we occasionally look a fool. They may be the best conduits for developing into the more confident, less self-conscious people we crave to be.

Useful foreign phrases

The big problem with the airport
is that we tend to go there when
we have a plane to catch.
As a result, we are panicked,
argumentative, stressed and
entirely unable to notice that we're
passing through one of the most
rewarding and interesting zones
of the modern world.

9.
The Pleasure of the Airport

The problem with the airport is that we tend to go there when we have a plane to catch. As a result, we are panicked, argumentative, stressed and entirely unable to notice that we're passing through one of the most rewarding and interesting zones of the modern world. We should make it a destination in its own right.

There are the beginnings of a thousand novels all around the departure lounge. Some of the trips commencing here will have been decided upon only in the previous few days, booked in response to a swiftly developing situation in the Munich or Milan office; others will be the fruit of three years of painful anticipation of a return to a village in northern Kashmir, with six dark-green suitcases filled with gifts for young relatives whom one has not yet met.

Nowhere is the airport's appeal more concentrated than in the television screens placed at intervals across terminals, which announce, in unromantic fonts, the itineraries of aircraft about to take to the skies. The screens imply a feeling of infinite and immediate possibility: they suggest the ease with which we might impulsively approach a ticket desk and, within a few hours, embark for a country where the call to prayer rings out over shuttered whitewashed houses, where we understand nothing of the language and where no one knows our identities. The lack of detail about the destinations serves only to stir unfocused images of nostalgia and longing: Rome, Tripoli, Nice, St Petersburg, Miami, Muscat via Abu Dhabi, Algiers, Kiev, Grand Cayman via Nassau – all of these destinations are like enemies of despair, to which we might appeal at moments of claustrophobia and stagnation, when home has become too much.

We forget how extraordinary and peculiar air travel can be. Yesterday we had chicken inasal for lunch at a crowded open air stall in the humid heat by the Guimaras Strait, and later this morning we'll be sat at gate 42 at Heathrow eating a bacon and egg roll while we wait for our connecting flight to Glasgow, where it's currently -2°C.

Arrivals can be hellish, of course, but despite the exhaustion, your senses are on fire, registering everything – the light, the signage, the skin tones, the metallic sounds, the advertisements – as if you were on drugs or a newborn baby – or Tolstoy. It is like being reborn. How peculiar this morning light seems against the memory of dawn in the Obudu hills. How unusual the recorded announcements after the wind in the High Atlas.

We should never give up this perspective. We should want to keep in mind everything we've learnt of alternative realities, as we have seen them in Tunis or Hyderabad, Lima or St Gallen. We should never forget that nothing here is normal, that the streets are different in Valletta and Luoyang, that this is only one of many possible worlds.

Despite its (often well-deserved) appalling reputation, the airport is – in its own way – trying to teach us a range of very important things.

10.
The Pleasure of the Flight

It's strange, being up here, pressed against the window. To the side, a pair of engines, their immense labours concealed within their gently rounded casing. In modest lettering they announce their limited, but precise demands: that we avoid walking on the wing from which they are suspended and that we do not attempt to pour anything other than oil into their small apertures. Later they will be tended by a team of engineers, currently sleeping, in a service hanger on another continent.

In the cabin, there is not much talk about the clouds that are visible up here. No one thinks it remarkable that somewhere above an ocean we flew past a vast white candy-floss island which would have made a perfect seat for an angel or even God himself in a painting by Piero della Francesca. No one leaps to their feet to announce with requisite emphasis that, out of the window, we are flying over a cloud, a matter that would have amazed Leonardo and Poussin, Claude and Constable.

The world feels large and we very small – and the contrast is delightful. On this scale, the actions and concerns of our own lives don't really count for much. We're beautifully reminded of our own thorough unimportance.

Across history, people have imagined their gods living on lofty mountaintops or in the sky, looking down benignly on human life. It's not a random association: from this height we can smile gently at humanity and perhaps love it a little, too. Even the grimmer areas of urban sprawl look serene and beautifully organised: the eastern suburbs of Glasgow nestle among wide tracts of farmland;

microscopic lorries work their way placidly towards the docks of Hamburg along elegant ribbons of autobahn.

The view helps us to have more kindly thoughts about those left back at home. Their faults drop away against the backdrop of the Southern Alps or the Singapore Strait. We want to be patient and warm around them. We see the broader outlines of their lives. We'd like to tell them in franker, more direct terms how fond we are of them.

Lunch arrives; we spear a tiny roasted potato or a small piece of fish and prise the foil top off a squat carton of orange juice as we pass over a region where, four miles below on the ground, we would need to travel in an armed convoy. Later we pad along the aisle to explore the lavatory, wearing the shapeless socks the airline has provided. Perhaps at this moment a team of climbers are encamped below the summit of a ferocious mountain, bracing themselves for a final assault on the ice walls and overhangs – while we carefully dry our hands and think of watching a comedy on our seat-back screen.

The physical world – against which our ancestors struggled – has been tamed; our little tube of alloy and glass slips calmly over the forests, deserts and oceans that thwarted and terrified them.

As we start the descent, helped by the complex manoeuvres of the plane through the lower atmosphere, we dream of becoming the people we long to be. We'll be energetic but thoughtful; sensitive but adventurous; we'll eat modestly, appreciate our circumstances and remain committed to doing our best with the time that remains to us.

11.
Pretty Cities

The majority of our days are spent on ugly streets. Ever since the development of concrete, steel and plastic, monstrosities have become the norm. Most of our cities are furiously ugly.

One (optimistic) view is that this might not matter very much. Perhaps we can be the same sort of people wherever we happen to be; the colour of the bricks or the design of windows surely leave the fundamentals of life unchanged.

And yet, as our travels show, we crave architectural and civic beauty, because we intuitively appreciate how much we are at the mercy of our architectural environments. We know we aren't the same people wherever we go. In the middle of Frankfurt, Milton Keynes or Detroit, the ugliness hacks away at our souls. And in Trieste or Portland, Seville or Florence, our benign personalities expand

It would be a good deal easier if we could remain in much the same mood wherever we happened to be. It is maddening how vulnerable we are to the coded messages that emanate from buildings. In the best cities, the streets whisper of hope, dignity, community and friendship. They invite us to become the noblest versions of ourselves.

If we better understood the impact that ugly architecture has on our lives, its power to sap our spirits and give assistance to our worst selves, we'd surely legislate against it. But as yet, no politician who announced an intention to make the built environment more beautiful would prosper – or even be deemed sane.

In utopia, architecture would more fairly be interpreted as a branch of mental health, with a crucial role to play in public contentment. And bad design would – at last – be interpreted as the crime it is to the health of the collective spirit.

Until then, it is to travel – and the intelligent, soul-stirring streets of San Gimignano or Kyoto, Jaipur or Yangon – that we must direct our longings.

For all the talk of globalisation, places retain a fascinating, welcome distinctiveness. The smells, the sounds, the bread, the light at dawn, people's shoes, the way of making tea, the arrangements of the taps and sockets, the light at 5pm…

12.
The Pleasure of Otherness

Only a few hours ago, you were at home; now you're here, in the souk in the Old Medina in Casablanca. There's a man, who must be a decade older than you, sitting on a worn leather stool in a little booth selling pistachios, preserved lemons and harissa paste. This might have been his life for the last twenty years or so. His radio is playing music by someone you don't recognise, but who is probably a huge star, with a powerful voice that soars as she repeats a word that sounds like 'eleh'. You've travelled a long way to go and see the Hassan II Mosque. For him, it's just a typical backdrop to ordinary life – as familiar and unremarkable as your queen's palace might be to you.

Or you're in the German capital, in a small bar in Kreuzberg, around the corner from the hotel you've just checked into; it's quite busy, even though it's the middle of the afternoon. There are candles lit on all the wonky tables; next to you, a good-looking couple are having an intense conversation in which the words *Kultur* and *Philosophie* keep getting stressed; a middle-aged woman is immersed in a thick book (about Schopenhauer) and taking rapid notes; at quiet moments the bartender is skimming through a newspaper – *Die Zeit* – which, you notice, features a large mathematical equation on the front page.

What we can feel at such moments is a basic pleasure at encountering 'otherness': practices, customs, habits and vocabularies that are strikingly at odds with those we know from home and which give us a welcome reminder of the sheer diversity and complexity of the world. From a settled vantage point, it's only too easy to picture humanity as homogeneous and, therefore, a little dull and prescriptive. But this isn't a view which can survive the first few hours in a new country. We're quickly reminded that, for all the talk of globalisation, places retain a fascinating, welcome distinctiveness. The smells, the sounds, the bread, the light at dawn, people's shoes, the way of making tea, the arrangements of the taps and sockets, the light at 5pm... everything is satisfyingly 'other'. This can become an invitation to explore alternative ways of living and thinking. There may be many more routes to being happy than the ones we've explored to date. Perhaps we can make the changes that had felt so impossible before.

All this the pistachio-seller is subtly helping us to remember. We might buy a packet or two from him to cement the lesson.

13.
The Longing to Talk to Strangers

The tourist industry has been spectacularly successful at opening up foreign countries and introducing us to their most important and worthwhile attractions.

Except for one extraordinary omission: the people. By some unseen, undiscussed but all-powerful rule, tourism tends to separate us from the inhabitants of the countries we've come to visit. They remain shadowy, occasional figures: the guy by the pool, the taxi driver from the airport, the nice lady who took us on the trip through the forest. But the real focus is always elsewhere, on the culture and the monuments, the natural spectacles and the food.

This is a source of serious sadness. Most of the places we want to travel to are associated with a distinctive way of being: an implicit personality. In New York, it might be confidence and modernity; in Amsterdam, the dignity of daily life; in Melbourne, a welcome directness and warmth. It's a range of human virtues that draw us to places, but we're normally only permitted to encounter these via their external, cultural expressions. We don't really want to shop or see pictures; we want to talk.

Yet we remain – painfully – outsiders. We pass a big family celebration at a long table on a café terrace. Someone is singing a song to which everyone knows the words. We scan the properties for sale in the windows of estate agents and picture ourselves moving in. We observe people after work catching trains and buses home to areas we know nothing of. We're continually noticing interesting faces, styles of clothing, the gestures friends use when they greet one another. In the evening, we hear the sounds of a party filtering down from a brightly lit third-floor flat. We may have explored every painting this country made in the eighteenth century and become experts at the late medieval style of its temples, but we're only scratching the surface of its being. The *genius loci* – the spirit of the place – is eluding us. We want to know what it would be like – if only for a few days – to join in and belong; and to try out for ourselves the nicest aspects of the attitudes and point of view of the people who live here.

In the travel industry of the future, we'll regard booking a local friend as no different from booking a hotel room or a flight: just another essential, normal part of organising a successful trip.

Until then, we must develop our skills at courageously going up to strangers and sharing a thought on the weather or the state of local politics. Or else we can remain in our shy cocoon, but should at least interpret our melancholy feelings as symptoms of an industry-wide failure, not a personal curse.

14.
The Vulnerability of Perfection
to Emotional Troubles

The tourist industry spends a lot of time assuring us that the more money we spend, the happier we will be.

The equation often seems deeply convincing – and, sometimes, if resources allow, we do as we've been told. We select a truly stunning location right on the ocean or in a fashionable district that used to be full of factories and is now dotted with stylish boutiques. The hotel has very nice bedside lamps, fine art on the walls and a luxurious marble bathroom. The service is impeccable. We secure a succession of tables at well-reviewed restaurants. We arrange a sleek car to meet us at the airport. There are endless attractions for the children. We pay for a tennis teacher. We feel deeply fortunate: we are going to have the holiday of a lifetime.

But amidst all this expenditure, we're liable to have neglected a crucial component of human contentment. All capacity for satisfaction depends first and foremost upon emotional well-being. The slightest psychological disturbance can destroy the benefits of a multi-billion-dollar hotel and chauffeured automobile. If our partner makes a snide comment, it won't matter how celebrated the *homard au champagne* happens to be; the delicate richness of its flavour will count for very little when we've been the victim of a sarcastic remark about our career potential. A grumpy thirteen-year-old child can single-handedly negate the efforts of an entire team of gardeners or museum curators. Or if the person we are with won't have sex with us in the way we really want, it will be no consolation that some small tubes of conditioner in the vicinity have been personally selected by Donatella Versace or that a handmade Belgian chocolate truffle was placed on the pillow into which we now feel like weeping deeply.

Regarded from an immense, impersonal distance, these are comic eventualities; close up they feel more like tragedies. This isn't an argument against luxury – just an analysis of its limitations. The same sorrows might easily come our way on a shoestring budget. We're not encountering the irrelevance of spending a great deal of money on travel: only the centrality and primacy of emotional satisfaction within the total economy of happiness.

The family holiday has little to do with the destination or the thrills of the itinerary: it lies in the capacity of a trip to cement the bonds of affection between family members; in the power of a trip to make a family.

15.
The Importance of
Family Holidays

It's because we're all such intuitive experts in knowing how they can go wrong that it's worth remembering what – at their best – family holidays can achieve. The point has little to do with the destination or the thrills of the itinerary: it lies in the capacity of a trip to cement the bonds of affection between family members; in the power of a trip to make a family.

For a start, trips erase the normal hierarchy between generations. A child gets to see their parents in unfamiliar – and often usefully less than impressive – situations. A father looks awkward in swimming trunks, a bulging stomach no longer disguised by a carefully fitted suit; or a mother – who is normally effortlessly in charge – is revealed as rather shy when it comes to trying to order from a foreign menu. With their frailties and limitations more on show, parents are humanised. A father turns out to be very nervous about being splashed in the pool, a mother is useless at building sandcastles. A child has a chance to be a parental equal or superior. When it comes to manoeuvring a rowing boat into the jetty or buying tomatoes at the market, a ten-year-old might be as adept as – or more skilled than – a parent; there's a new, welcome experience of equality.

There are associated benefits in experiencing danger together: in being caught out in a rainstorm after the museum, in getting lost in the bazaar, in needing to sort out a stolen wallet, in having to find somewhere to sleep at 11pm. At the time, these discomforts feel like an interruption of the real point of the trip. Only later do we realise that they are what helped us to get to know one another properly and overcome the egocentricity and reserve of home.

A trip is helpful, too, in allowing parents to see the world through the unjaded eyes of their children. The normal hierarchies of pleasure are upturned and new delights unearthed. The breakfast buffet at the hotel becomes thrilling in a way it otherwise never would, because for a five-year-old child, few things are as delightful as being allowed to carry a small plate around and choose freely from three kinds of bread and explore strange combinations of cheese and strawberries or a sausage and smoked salmon. The museum of art has nothing to rival this. In the company of children, we notice how conservative our adult sensibilities have become. We realise we have forgotten how enchanting a small lizard can be or how much fun is available from timing jumps over a succession of small waves.

When adolescence arrives, the family holiday often loses its sweetness; the child wants to remain at home or go out with their friends; it would be horrible to go for a walk along the beach with parents or join them on the tennis court. The death of the family holiday in adolescence is – ironically – quite probably the very earliest move towards a new epoch of family holidays, due to start in two decades' time or so. The rejection of the parents, which seems so harsh right now, is what will allow children, in turn, to have a family of their own one day – and eventually to end up doing all the things they currently most disdain. They'll be singing in the paddling pool and pretending their ice cream is too hot; they'll make unfunny jokes with the best will in the world and won't care very much that there's a coffee stain on their ill-fitting T-shirt. They too will come to learn the invaluable benefits of a family trip away.

16.
The Pleasure of the
Romantic Minibreak

One of the stranger aspects of relationships is that we may, in order to sustain them, need to go away together every now and then.

In theory, it should make no difference to love quite where we happen to be. But in practice, the furniture may have to alter, so that we can. The familiar backdrop of home keeps us too tightly and punitively tethered to whom we have so often been – which may mean, to the less impressive and more unkind versions of ourselves. The sofa remembers that argument we once had on it; the kitchen keeps us connected to some unpleasant scenes that unfolded in it over too many evenings.

But the new surroundings have no such memories. They allow us to start afresh and rediscover wellsprings of affection and generosity. The minibreak isn't a chance to avoid conflict. It's an opportunity to have some of the discussions we really need to have, with enough time and kindness to deal with what we uncover. The problem with our rows at home isn't that they happen, but that we don't find the energy to get to the root of them.

We're carrying around a range of complaints. Perhaps they sounded too petty or humiliating to mention at the time. But when they fester, the currents of affection start to get blocked – and soon, we may find ourselves flinching when our partner tries to touch us. What we call 'loss of desire' is usually simply a kind of anger with a partner that hasn't had a chance to understand itself.

The holiday is a safe moment in which to reveal some of these – typically entirely unintentional – hurts. It is a chance, too, for gratitude. The partner has brought us so much we've forgotten to thank them for. They have made it possible to do things we'd never have accomplished on our own; they've comforted us at certain moments, they've maybe understood and been kind to difficult aspects of who we are; possibly they have saved us from the worst effects of some specific tendencies in our nature.

With the help of a trip away, we can jog our memories and help each other to come to a fairer, more precise view of our lives together.

17.
The Little Restaurant

Almost all of us are, when we travel, in search of this ideal establishment: the little restaurant. Let's picture it for ourselves. It's fairly small, ten or a dozen tables. It's unpretentious; the floor and the walls are quite bare and the chairs simple in the extreme. The place has no anxiety about itself. It knows it does its job well and has no need to be ingratiating with its customers. The grilled fish is good enough for the lightbulbs on the wall to be left exposed without shame. The menu is extremely short, and perhaps chalked up on a blackboard by the till every day. Everything is simple, fresh, yet absolutely remarkable. It comes quickly, the waiters are friendly and unfussy, the water comes in an old wine bottle – and the bill, when it arrives, is very modest indeed. As we pay, we think to ourselves that this truly is the perfect restaurant.

The problem is that such places are woefully rare. Every traveller is in search of such an establishment and yet they are as elusive as gold dust. Why are we, collectively, not better at making little restaurants?

The romantic answer is that these businesses are the result of genius, and cannot be made to spring up in large numbers. But that cannot be true. The reality is that the lovely little restaurant isn't a chance aberration; it's founded on a set of reasonable, logical and teachable ideas about what makes people happy. If we understood ourselves and human nature a little better, there could conceivably be countless such 'locals'.

Through the prism of the little restaurant, we meet with a big truth about travel: we're not very good at understanding what really makes us content. Our answers tend towards the expensive, the grandiose,

the sentimental and the kitsch. We aren't good at working back from what we really enjoyed and then designing businesses that can cater to it.

If we were cannier about our pleasures, we'd ensure that we spent more time chatting with people and less time in museums; that we'd be less seduced by whale-watching trips and more alert to the interest of walking around foreign supermarkets.

And we'd grasp that we were less interested in the grand and ornate brasserie, and more attuned to the distinctive charms of the little restaurant. Going travelling collides us repeatedly with a big, difficult, but also in a sense rather exciting idea: that we're collectively still at the dawn of knowing how to make ourselves properly happy.

18.

In Defence of Crowds

It's fashionable, of course, to hate crowds. Good travellers are always complaining about them. Perhaps we ascended Mount Pilatus in Switzerland early in the morning and were disgusted to find that there were already several dozen people at the summit, or we went to Athens to look at the Parthenon and we were appalled by how many groups were wandering about the ruins.

Our distress is very real. But if we examine our annoyance in detail, it turns out that it's not actually the presence of lots of other people that is bothering us so much. Crucially, there are certain occasions when we have a powerfully positive experience of being in a crowd. If we're attending – for instance – the Olympic Opening Ceremony, it's deeply thrilling to feel that we're sharing moments of collective pride with many others in an atmosphere of dignity and prowess. Or, if we're at a religious service in a cathedral, the grandeur and solemnity of the occasion is profoundly enhanced by the fact that thousands of people are at the same time rising to their feet and singing a hymn, or simultaneously contemplating the errors of their lives and seeking forgiveness for the wrongs they have all done to one another.

Keeping such experiences in mind shows us that it's rarely the pure quantity of other human beings that upsets us: it's something else. It is the lack of a sense of nobility, ceremony or shared occasion. It could be one of life's most majestic experiences to be gathered on a mountain top with a multitude of others in a moment of joint awe and humility at the sight of the world spread below us; it could be deeply moving to be part of a mass of people who gathered around the broken columns of an ancient Greek temple dedicated to the goddess of wisdom.

Knowing this can't, by itself, solve our problem with crowds. But it shows us more accurately what's bothering us when we travel: we don't hate people, we're just missing the sense of dignified shared devotion. We don't really need every place to ourselves. We want there to be a crowd – only of a different kind.

On a densely populated planet, the ideal of being alone is very understandable – but it has grown ever more problematic. All the very interesting and attractive places get busy. The desire to journey away from the crowd simply leads us to a desperate scramble for ever more remote locations: the Galápagos Islands, the ice shelves of Alaska and (most exclusive of all) outer space; places which will, in turn, get spoilt too.

However, the grander and more hopeful ambition is to transform our experience of being one of many; to turn the idea of a group from an insult to a virtue: to make belonging as nice as it can be.

The desire to journey away from the crowd simply leads us to a desperate scramble for ever more remote locations: the Galápagos Islands, the ice shelves of Alaska and (most exclusive of all) outer space; places which will, in turn, get spoilt too.

19.
The Pleasure of Room Service

It's not a very respectable pleasure, but it's a powerful one all the same. You pick up the phone, balancing the in-room dining menu on your knee, you nip into the shower and flick on the news and half an hour later someone comes to your room with a tray, or wheels a trolley to the foot of the bed. The meal itself might not be anything terribly special – chicken schnitzel or macaroni and cheese – but it's surrounded by signs of care. They've kept it warm in a special heated recess under the table or covered it under a small metallic dome; someone has wondered if we might like flowers, and has inserted a tulip into a narrow glass vase to cheer us as we eat; they've worried that we might be fussy about bread and provided a small selection; they'd like to know if we prefer still or sparking water.

They don't always get it right. But their thoughtfulness is touchingly evident. It's such a poignant contrast to how things often go at home: your child doesn't even look up when you say good morning; your partner grunts when you mention that you had a tricky day at work; at parties you catch them speaking in a rather dismissive, offhand way about what an idiot you generally are.

It's not surprising if – as we sit on the bed half-naked in our dressing gown and bite into an apple strudel – we are genuinely moved. It's all artifice of course – engineered by payment. But thanks to an item on the credit card bill, we can get something truly lovely: a portion of the kindness we crave, but hardly ever receive.

Money won't buy what we most want: the warm regard of those we live with. But we can get at least a symbol of considerateness, and sometimes that might be the best we can hope for in our broken, radically imperfect lives.

20.
The Pleasures of Nature

One of the most consoling aspects of travel is that we are likely to encounter nature in a way we don't in the rest of our lives. Natural phenomena – it might be the ocean, a sheep, a forest or a valley – have nothing whatsoever to do with our own perilous and tortured human priorities. They are redemptively unconcerned with everything we are and want. They implicitly mock our self-importance and self-absorption and so return us to a fairer, more modest sense of our role on the planet.

A sheep doesn't know about our feelings of jealousy; it has no interest in our humiliation and bitterness around a colleague; it has never emailed. On a walk in the hills, it simply ambles towards the path we're on and looks curiously at us, then takes a lazy mouthful of grass, chewing from the side of its mouth as though it were chewing gum. One of its companions approaches and sits next to it, wool to wool, and for a second, they exchange what appears to be a knowing, mildly amused glance.

Beyond the sheep are a couple of oak trees. They are of especially noble bearing; they gather their lower branches tightly under themselves while their upper branches grow in small orderly steps, producing a rich green foliage in an almost perfect circle. It doesn't matter if there's an election or what happens to the stock market or in the final exams. The same patterns of growth would have been going on when Napoleon was leading his armies across Europe or when the first nomads made their way towards the Appalachian hills.

Our encounter with nature calms us because none of our troubles, disappointments or hopes has any relevance to it. Everything that happens to us, or that we do, is of no consequence whatever from the point of view of the ocean, the sheep, the trees, the clouds or the stars; they are deeply important representatives of an entirely different perspective within which our own concerns are mercifully irrelevant.

21.
Drawing Rather than
Taking Photographs

Whenever something looks interesting or beautiful, there's a natural impulse to want to capture and preserve it – which means, in this day and age, that we're likely to reach for our phones to take a picture. Though this would seem to be an ideal solution, there are two big problems associated with taking pictures. Firstly, we're likely to be so busy taking the pictures, we forget to look at the world whose beauty and interest prompted us to take a photograph in the first place. And secondly, because we feel the pictures are safely stored on our phones, we never get around to looking at them, so sure are we that we'll get around to it one day.

These problems would seem to be very much of today, a consequence of the tiny phones in our pockets. But they were noticed right at the beginning of the history of photography, when the average camera was the size of a grandfather clock. The first person to notice them was the English art critic, John Ruskin. He was a keen traveller who realised that most tourists make a dismal job of noticing or remembering the beautiful things they see. He argued that humans have an innate tendency to respond to beauty and a desire to possess it, but that there are better and worse expressions of this desire. At worst, we get into buying souvenirs or taking photographs. But, in Ruskin's eyes, there's one thing we should do and that is attempt to draw the interesting things we see, irrespective of whether we happen to have any talent for doing so.

Before the invention of photography, people used to draw far more than they do today. It was an active necessity. But in the mid-nineteenth century, photography killed drawing. It became something only 'artists' would ever do, so Ruskin – passionate promoter of drawing and enemy of the camera – spent four years on a campaign to get people sketching again. He wrote books, gave speeches and funded art schools, but he saw no paradox in stressing that his campaign had nothing to do with getting people to draw well: 'A man is born an artist as a hippopotamus is born a hippopotamus; and you can no more make yourself one than you can make yourself a giraffe.'

So, if drawing had value even when it was practised by people with no talent, it was – for Ruskin – because drawing can teach us to see: to notice properly rather than gaze absentmindedly. In the process of recreating with our own hand what lies before our eyes, we naturally move from a position of observing beauty in a loose way to one where we acquire a deep understanding of its parts.

Ruskin was very distressed by how seldom people notice details. He deplored the blindness and haste of modern tourists, especially those who prided themselves on covering Europe in a week by train (a service first offered by Thomas Cook in 1862):

> No changing of place at a hundred miles an hour will make us one whit stronger, happier, or wiser. There was always more in the world than men could see, walked they ever so slowly; they will see it no better for going fast. The really precious things are thought and sight, not pace. It does a bullet no good to go fast; and a man, if he be truly a man, no harm to go slow; for his glory is not at all in going, but in being.

So he slowed things down and recommended we spend far longer looking at impressive things, even quite simple things. His own drawings showed the way.

It is a measure of how accustomed we are to rushing that we would be thought unusual and perhaps dangerous if we stopped and stared at a place for as long as a sketcher would require to draw it. Ten minutes of acute concentration at least are needed to draw a tree; the prettiest tree rarely stops passers-by for longer than a minute.

We should dare to give drawing a go.

Study of a Peacock's Breast Feather,
John Ruskin, 1875

No changing of place at a hundred miles an hour will make us one whit stronger, happier, or wiser. There was always more in the world than men could see, walked they ever so slowly; they will see it no better for going fast.

Give drawing a go

22.
Holiday Fling

Of course the idea of a short-lived holiday romance can sound rather crass or emotionally exploitative. But there's potentially a good version that links falling in love (even though we know it probably won't last) to the best ambitions of travel. The ideal lessons that a destination might offer to teach us are not fully contained in its history or its public monuments and museums. They are encoded in the lives of the people who live there: in the way they see the world, in their attitudes to work, to each other, to family.

Romance becomes valid and important as an aspect of tourism because of the way it rapidly deepens a relationship to another person and thereby a place. As we kiss, we overcome the distancing layers of conventional politeness that so often get in the way of encountering another individual. We move to a higher level of communication.

It's not the physical intimacy itself that really matters. It's all the other things that happen around it: late into the night, they tell us the inside story of their childhood and how their parents met; we go with them to their local supermarket to get something for lunch; we hear about the troubles of their friends; we get to know their ambitions and their worries. Perhaps the most poignant moment is when they unlock their front door: we pass out of the street that anyone can walk along and enter their private world. We get to see the places that are usually closed off from the tourist. We hear about their schooldays and what it was like looking for work. They tell us about their boss and their colleagues.

All these details educate us. What can grandly be called the 'spirit of the place' – the thing that we've travelled to meet – stops being an abstract, intellectual notion. It becomes more tangible and more specific; it's earthed. We're not just looking for random company: we want to meet an individual who properly represents the virtues of their locality. It might seem foolish to connect with someone so intensely for such a brief moment when we know they live hundreds of miles and several time zones away from us and yet, when things go right, we may really be doing, in the most direct and profound way, the very thing that we came here to do: learning and growing through contact with important virtues and attitudes that are missing in ourselves.

23.
Travelling for Perspective

There's a long tradition of going travelling in search of things we lack. In the eighteenth century, well-off young English men would take trips to Paris and Rome to acquire more elegant manners and study Classical history; today we might travel to find sunshine or nature.

But there are many things we struggle with beyond our inability to understand Roman culture or endure a long, wet winter – and travel can help us with them. A central issue is that we are constantly at risk of feeling disenchanted with our circumstances. At a personal level, we are continually exposed to the enviable lives of others; our imaginations are haunted by our comparative lack of success. At a more general level, our societies often appear fundamentally unimpressive: our institutions look compromised, our media seems coarse and sensationalist, our cities feel chaotic. There is, apparently, little to be grateful for.

In theory – of course – we know that can't be entirely true. We know, in the abstract, that we're lucky to have enough to eat and a roof over our heads. But such reminders feel emotionally unreal and usually have little impact on their own.

For the truth to hit home, we may have to immerse ourselves in true poverty and a genuinely dysfunctional society. We may need to travel to the large parts of the world where people live, on average, on $500 a year or less.

We may need to visit a place where it's normal for the police to extort money from you; where a newspaper editor is likely to be arrested for criticising authority; where government is self-evidently tied to violence and corruption; where the opposition is an armed faction; where a fair trial is a rarity; where luxury would be clean sheets or a tube of toothpaste; where there might be excrement in your food or a dead rat under your bed. A city or country where people maddened by toothache pull out their own teeth; where horrendous infections are commonplace; where large numbers of children receive almost no formal education; where, if there is a school, it is quite probable that those in charge are syphoning off the funds; where sewers run openly through the streets; where people spend their days picking over the refuse in huge dumps.

We may well end up deeply moved. As importantly, we are invited to change our perceptions of our own lives, to renew our appreciation of so much that we'd taken for granted: a toilet that flushes, a washing machine, space to ourselves, a pleasant lunch. And we may derive a new sense of how profound and powerful the achievements of our own societies – for all their failings – really are.

Paradoxical though it sounds, travels to places where the true hardships of existence are grimly evident can provide a needed education in gratitude. Our encounter with the reality of the lives of so many others pushes us towards a more accurate perspective on our own condition. Like many great artworks in elegant galleries, they teach us to see – and admire – aspects of the world we usually inhabit that we had scarcely noticed before. And they do this with rather more conviction and lasting impact than any canvas on a wall.

856

24.
Travel and Pilgrimages

Religions have shown a surprising degree of sympathy for our impulse to travel. They have accepted that we cannot achieve everything by staying at home. They've also taken travel very seriously, far more seriously than we do now; they've interpreted it as a major way to be healed.

In Christianity, the point of a pilgrimage was to visit a shrine of a long-dead saint and there beg for a cure for a variety of physical and mental ailments. Every ailment called for contact with a specific holy place, of which there were a confusing multitude scattered across Europe. France alone offered mothers having trouble lactating a choice of forty-six sanctuaries of Mary's Holy Breast Milk ('Had the Virgin been a cow,' observed the sixteenth-century Protestant John Calvin unkindly, 'she scarcely could not have produced such a quantity.'). Atlases of pilgrimages were like complex apothecaries: believers with a painful molar were advised to travel to Rome to the Basilica of San Lorenzo, where they would touch the arm bones of St Apollonia, the patron saint of teeth or, if such a trip were awkward, they might go and find pieces of her jaw in the Jesuit church at Antwerp, some of her hair at St Augustine's in Brussels, or her toes at disparate sites around Cologne. Unhappily married women were directed to travel to Umbria to touch the shrine of St Rita of Cascia, patron saint of marital problems (and lost causes). Soldiers looking to embolden themselves before a battle could commune with the bones of St Foy in a gold-plated reliquary in the abbey church in Conques in southwestern France – while people who worried excessively about lightning could gain relief by travelling to the Jesuit church in Bad Muenstereifel in Germany and laying hands on the relics of St Donatus, believed to offer help against fires and explosions of all kinds.

Though we no longer believe in the divine power of journeys to cure toothache or gall stones, and though most of the problems motivating pilgrimages are now more appropriately addressed by a visit to a clinic, we can still hang on to the idea that certain parts of the world possess a power to address our ills. There are places that, by virtue of their remoteness, vastness, climate, chaotic energy, haunting melancholy or sheer difference from our homelands exert a capacity to salve the wounded parts of us. These sites, valuable rather than holy, help us to recover perspective, reorder our ambitions, quell our paranoias and remind us of the interest and obliging unexpectedness of life.

Though we intuit this at a general level, we lack, as yet, a tradition of approaching travel from a properly therapeutic perspective and so of analysing landscapes according to their benefits to our souls. We lack atlases of destinations with which to treat our worries and sorrows.

The Christian Church kept a tight grip both on where pilgrims went, and on what they did and thought about each day as they made their way there. It sought to buttress otherwise fleeting and forgettable sensations by giving pilgrims prayers and songs, it urged them regularly and publicly to rehearse their motives for travelling and it equipped them with distinctive garments to help them mentally separate themselves from their ordinary lives.

Medieval travel was slow at the best of times, but committed pilgrims went out of their way to make it even slower, forgoing the use of river barges or horses in favour of their own feet. A pilgrimage from northern Europe to the remains of St James the Apostle in Santiago could take eight months, pilgrims leaving in the spring and not making it back before the onset of winter.

Pilgrims were not being perverse in their insistence on slowness and difficulty. They were aware that one of our central motives for travelling is a desire to put the regrettable aspects of the past behind us, a desire explicitly recognised in the Christian notion of the pilgrimage as a penance. Furthermore, they knew that one of the most effective ways of achieving a feeling of distance from follies, vanity and sinfulness is to introduce something very large – like the experience of a month-long journey across a desert or a mountain range – between our past and our desired future. Our attempts at inner transition can be cemented by a protracted and hazardous progress. If inner change is difficult, then we may need a commensurately difficult outer journey to inspire and goad us.

Whatever the advantages of plentiful, swift and relatively convenient air travel, we may curse it for being, in the end, not painful or slow enough – and so for subverting our attempts to draw a convincing line under the past.

The travel industry should not be allowed to escape the underlying seriousness of the area of life it has been assigned to oversee. We need to relearn how to use travel as a way of being existentially healed, rather than merely entertained or tanned.

25.

HOW TO

SPEND A FEW DAYS

IN PARIS

Paris is one of the world's most famous and visited cities. How should we spend a couple of days there? In trying to answer this, we'll simultaneously be examining some big questions about travel more generally.

Often a trip to Paris is organised around a homage to culture. We want to get in touch with great cultural figures: we go to see their works and the places they lived and worked. We're trying to get close to them. But there's a strange irony: one of the things these people would never have done is visit museums. We would be better off focusing on what they loved, not what they made or where they hung out.

For instance, we might want to honour the eighteenth-century painter Chardin by going to the Louvre and looking at some of his paintings.

The Silver Cup, Chardin, c.1768.

But Chardin didn't spend his time doing that: he had little interest in exhibitions. What he liked doing was going to the market and buying apples and looking at them carefully.

We might be inclined to make a trip to the café de Flore at the intersection of boulevard Saint-Germain and rue Saint-Benoît in order to see the place where Jean-Paul Sartre did a lot of his philosophical writing.

Jean-Paul Sartre and writer Simone de Beauvoir
having lunch at a café in Paris, 1964.

At the back of our minds, perhaps, we hope that by seeing the place we'll boost our own creative and intellectual life. That's a very nice and important goal. But there's something curious about the way we're pursuing it. Sartre went to that café because it happened to be a pleasant stroll from where he lived and (at the time) it was cheap and convenient. He didn't himself visit cafés to see where other writers had had lunch. To be closer to him in spirit we should do what he did: go to any modestly priced café we quite like that's near to where we're staying and work on our own ideas.

It could seem rather interesting – if one is literary-minded – to pay a visit to a recreation at the Musée Carnavalet of Marcel Proust's bedroom: the cork walled room where he wrote much of his great novel, *In Search of Lost Time*.

Marcel Proust's bedroom, as recreated
at the Musée Carnavalet, Paris.

However, this isn't something that would ever have particularly appealed to Proust himself. What he wanted to do was to stay in his own bedroom and think in great detail about his childhood, and he would have encouraged us to do the same. The true place to commune with Proust is back in our own little rented apartment.

Most visitors to Paris drop in to Notre-Dame.

The people who built it wanted us to come. But they weren't hoping that we'd be impressed by its pioneering use of flying buttresses or by the gargoyle water spouts high up on the roof. They primarily wanted us to examine our consciences and feel sorry for the wrong we have done to others; they wanted us to be generous to the needy and to wonder about the point of human existence.

Notre-Dame Cathedral, Paris.

These are experiences we can come by – perhaps more readily – in other places. Maybe by visiting one of the less famous graveyards, such as the Passy Cemetery, where the brevity of life is grimly apparent and where the hurts and preoccupations of our lives are put in true perspective.

Passy Cemetery in the
16th arrondissement of Paris.

Maybe we'd go to the Musée d'Orsay to see Claude Monet's painting *La Gare Saint-Lazare*, which he painted in 1877.

La Gare Saint-Lazare, Claude Monet, 1877.

The irony is that Monet himself didn't go to the Musée d'Orsay to paint this work. He spent many hours at the most sophisticated transport hub he could find, contemplating the technical grandeur of modern life. If we want to love what Monet loved, we might make space in our visit to spend more time at Charles de Gaulle airport.

Charles de Gaulle airport.

None of the great Parisian cultural figures – around whom many trips to Paris revolve – went there on holiday. They were writing, thinking and painting in the place they happened to live. They were interested in things – the beauty of ordinary objects, the meaning of life, memories – that don't belong to any one particular place. Perhaps the ideal outcome of two days in Paris is the realisation that we may not need to visit Paris at all.

Going home is, usually, the very sad bit.
Does it have to be?

26.
How to Come Home

Going home is, usually, the very sad bit. Does it have to be?

Seated together on most planes are people with very different expectations of where they are going: for some this will be the start of a journey to a new land, whilst others are those returning home. The first group is filled with excitement; they have guidebooks, cameras and knots of anticipation. The second may be too sad to touch their in-flight trays. On the final descent, they gaze at the landscape with melancholy faces. They have only home to contemplate, with its banal associations. And yet the two groups are travelling to the very same place. Once they have crossed customs, they will have before them the same monuments, museums, landscapes and foods.

Why do we accord such privileges to foreign places, and such ready disdain to our own lands? Would it not be one of the greatest skills, the most helpful kind of practical wisdom, to know how to sample a little of the excitement about our own countries that travellers are able to locate there?

Receptivity or openness might be the chief characteristic of the traveller's mindset. As travellers, we approach new places with curiosity. We don't assume we know everything. We stand on traffic islands and in narrow streets, gawping at and admiring what the locals take to be strange, small details. We risk getting run over because we are intrigued by the roof of a government building or an inscription on a wall. We find a supermarket or hairdresser unusually fascinating. We dwell at length on the layout of a menu or the clothes of the presenters on the evening news. We are alive to the layers of a country's history beneath the present.

At home, on the other hand, we assume we've discovered most of what is interesting about the neighbourhood, simply by virtue of having lived there a long time. It seems so hard to imagine that there could be something novel to unearth in a place where we've spent our daily lives over many decades.

But consider how much you might notice if you walked out of the front door, and imagined you had never seen any of it before, if you pictured yourself as a foreigner from a far-off land newly disembarked from a long-haul flight.

Given the limits on how much we are able to travel (and its costs and side-effects), we should endeavour to try, before taking off for distant hemispheres, to notice what we have already so often seen close at hand but have learnt to neglect, because it is familiar. And when we despair at coming back, we should be goaded on by the thought that 'boring home' is always someone else's deeply exciting 'abroad'.

27.
The Advantages of
Staying at Home

Lying in bed late at night or waiting on the platform for the train home, we often daydream about where it would be nicer to be: perhaps the beaches of Goa, a little restaurant by a quiet canal in Venice, the highway near Big Sur or the Faroe Islands, far to the north of Scotland.

The desire to travel is, almost always, sparked by a picture or two: a couple of mental snapshots that encapsulate all that seems most alluring about a destination. A trip lasting many hours and costing what could be a small fortune may be initiated by nothing grander or more examined than one or two mental postcards.

We travel because of a background belief that, of course, the reality of a scene must be nicer than the evanescent mental images that take us there. But there is something about the way our minds work that we would do well to study before we ever pack a suitcase: mental images are momentary. That is, they last, at best, three seconds. When we imagine a scene, we imagine not a film, but that far briefer and in many ways far more forgiving medium, a picture.

And yet, we are never in a destination just for a moment, and that brute fact alone may be enough to cause grievous damage to the hopes that transport us far from home. We know the phenomenon well enough at the cinema. Imagine if in the course of a story, the screen were filled with a sublime view of ocean waves crashing against a craggy headland. We might sigh with desire at such splendour. But if the camera started to linger on the scene, we might rapidly grow twitchy. What is fabulous in increments of seconds can become properly maddening after half a minute. Two minutes in, we may be so irritated as to be ready to leave our seats.

It's not that we're ungrateful or shallow, rather that we absorb beauty quickly and then want to move on. Beauty is like a brilliant joke: we laugh, but don't need the comic element to be continuously replayed.

The lovely mental pictures that get us to travel are – in essence – hugely edited versions of what we actually encounter in any destination. We will, eventually, certainly see these pictures, but we will also see so much else, so much that is painful or boring, dispiriting or mundane: hours of footage of the stained airline seat ahead of us, the back of the taxi driver's head, the wall of the cheap hotel, a framed photograph of Marilyn Monroe on the wall of a little local restaurant...

Furthermore, there will always be something else on the lens between us and the destination we'd come for, something so tricky and oppressive as to undermine the whole purpose of having left home in the first place, namely: ourselves.

We will, by an unavoidable error, bring ourselves along to every destination we'd ever wanted to enjoy.

And that will mean bringing along so much of the mental baggage that makes being us so intolerably problematic day-to-day: all the anxiety, regret, confusion, guilt, irritability and despair. None of this smear of the self is there when we picture a trip from home. In the imagination, we can enjoy unsullied views. But there, at the foot of the golden temple or high up on the pine-covered mountain, we stand to find that there is so much of 'us' intruding on our vistas.

We ruin our trips through the fateful habit of taking ourselves along on them.

There's a tragi-comic irony at work: the vast labour of getting ourselves physically to a place won't necessarily get us any closer to the essence of what we'd been seeking. As airlines, hotel chains and travel magazines conspire never to tell us, in daydreaming of the ideal location, we may have already enjoyed the very best that any place has to offer us.

28.
Cherishing Memories

Throughout our lives, we spend a lot of time – and even more money engineering pleasant experiences. We book airline tickets, visit beaches, admire glaciers, watch elephants drinking...

In all this, the emphasis is almost always on the experience itself – which lasts a certain amount of time, and then is over. The idea of making a big deal of revisiting an experience in memory sounds a little strange – or simply sad.

We're not assiduous or devoted cultivators of our past experiences. We shove the nice things that have happened to us to the back of the cupboard of our minds and don't particularly expect to see them ever again. They happen, and then we're done with them.

They do sometimes come back to us unbidden. We're on a boring train ride to work, and suddenly an image of a beach at dusk comes to life. Or while we're having a bath, we remember climbing a flower-covered mountain with a friend a decade before. But little attention tends to get paid to such moments. We don't engineer regular encounters with them. We may feel we have to dismiss them as 'daydreaming' or 'thinking about nothing'.

But what if we were to alter the hierarchy of prestige a little and argue that regular immersion in our memories is a critical part of what can sustain and console us – and, not least, is perhaps the cheapest and most flexible form of entertainment. We should learn regularly to travel around our minds and think it almost as prestigious to sit at home and reflect on a trip we once took to an island with our imaginations as to trek to the island with our cumbersome bodies.

In our neglect of our memories, we are spoilt children, who squeeze only a portion of the pleasure from experiences and then toss them aside to seek new thrills. Part of why we feel the need for so many new experiences may simply be that we are so bad at absorbing the ones we have had.

To help us focus more on our memories, we need nothing technical. We certainly don't need a camera. There is a camera in our minds already: it is always on, it takes in everything we've ever seen. Huge chunks of experience are still there in our heads, intact and vivid, just waiting for us to ask ourselves leading questions like: 'Where did we go after we landed?' or 'What was the first breakfast like?'

When we can't sleep, when there's no Wi-Fi, we should always think of going on Memory Journeys. Our experiences have not disappeared, just because they are no longer unfolding right in front of our eyes. We can remain in touch with so much of what made them pleasurable simply through the art of evocation.

We talk endlessly of virtual-reality. Yet we don't need gadgets. We have the finest virtual reality machines already in our own heads. We can – right now – shut our eyes and travel into, and linger amongst, the very best and most consoling and life-enhancing bits of our past.

29.

THE SHORTEST TRIP:

GOING FOR A WALK

A WALK IS, IN A SENSE,

THE SMALLEST SORT OF JOURNEY

WE CAN EVER UNDERTAKE.

IT STANDS IN RELATION

TO A TYPICAL HOLIDAY AS

A BONSAI TREE DOES

TO A FOREST.

EVEN IF IT'S ONLY

AROUND THE BLOCK

A FEW MOMENTS IN THE PARK

THE HIGH STREET

THREE OAK TREES

TWO ROBINS

A RIVER

A GROCER'S SHOP

A WALK IS ALREADY

A JOURNEY

The need to go for a walk comes from the same place as the longing to take off to another country: with a desire to restart our minds. We sometimes cannot work it all out by staying rooted in one place. We have stared at the screen too long, we have been bumping into the same inner obstacles without progress, we have grown claustrophobic within ourselves.

That is why we need the sight of the three oak trees and two robins by the river or the maelstrom of the high street, where we linger outside a grocer's shop and wonder (inconclusively, yet again) what dragon fruit might taste like. The better part of our minds has a habit of getting exhausted and sterile. It is scared as well. Some of the most profound thoughts we need to grapple with have a potentially disturbing character. An inner censor tends to kick in and block the progress we were starting to make towards ideas that – though important and interesting – also presented marked threats to short-term peace.

While we walk, the mind is no longer on guard. We're not supposed to be doing much inside our heads; we're mainly occupied with following a path around a pond or checking out a row of shops. The ideas that have been half-forming at the back of our minds, ideas about what the true purpose of our lives might be and what we should do next, keep up their steady inward pressure – but now there is a lot less to stop them reaching full consciousness. We're not meant to be thinking and so – at last – we can think freely and courageously.

The rhythmic motion of an easy stride helps to separate us from the ruts of our current preoccupations and allows us to wander more freely though neglected regions of our inner landscape. Themes we'd lost touch with – childhood, an odd dream we had recently, a friend we haven't seen for years, a big task we had always told ourselves we'd undertake – float into attention. In physical terms, we're hardly going any distance at all, but we're crossing acres of mental territory.

A short while later, we're back at the office or at home once again. No one has missed us, or perhaps even noticed that we've been out. Yet we are subtly different: a slightly more complete, more visionary, courageous and imaginative version of the person we knew how to be – before we wisely went out journeying.

FOLLOW A PATH

WANDER

MORE

FREELY

THROUGH

THE NEGLECTED

REGIONS

OF YOUR

INNER

LANDSCAPE

HOME

'ALL OF MAN'S UNHAPPINESS COMES FROM HIS INABILITY TO STAY ALONE IN HIS ROOM.'

Blaise Pascal

30.

The Shortest Travel Quiz

1. In what ways was Pascal right?

....

....

....

....

....

....

....

2. And in what ways was he wrong – or at least a bit unfair?

....

....

....

....

....

....

....

....

Notes

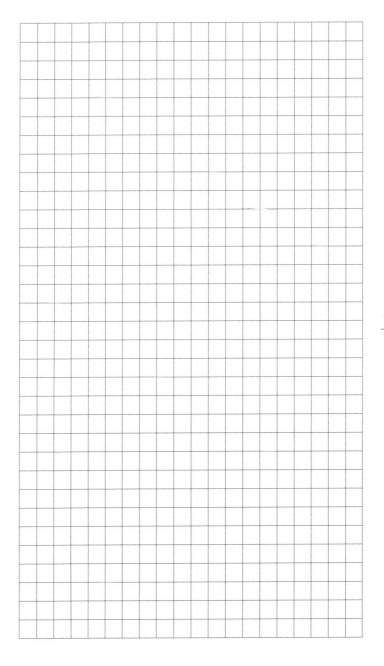

Picture credits

Published in 2018 by The School of Life
First published in the USA in 2019
930 High Road, London, N12 9RT
Copyright © The School of Life 2018

Designed and typeset by Marcia Mihotich
Printed in China by Leo Paper Group

A proportion of this book has appeared online at
www.theschooloflife.com/articles

Every effort has been made to contact the copyright holders
of the material reproduced in this book. If any have been
inadvertently overlooked, the publisher will be pleased to make
restitution at the earliest opportunity.

The School of Life publishes a range of books on essential topics
in psychological and emotional life, including relationships,
parenting, friendship, careers and fulfilment. The aim is always
to help us to understand ourselves better – and thereby to grow
calmer, less confused and more purposeful. Discover our full range
of titles, including books for children, here:
www.theschooloflife.com/books

The School of Life also offers a comprehensive therapy service,
which complements, and draws upon, our published works:
www.theschooloflife.com/therapy

ISBN 978-1-9999179-6-8

10 9 8 7 6

To join The School of Life community and find out more,
scan below:

The School of Life publishes a range of books on essential topics in psychological and emotional life, including relationships, parenting, friendship, careers and fulfilment. The aim is always to help us to understand ourselves better and thereby to grow calmer, less confused and more purposeful. Discover our full range of titles, including books for children, here:

www.theschooloflife.com/books

The School of Life also offers a comprehensive therapy service, which complements, and draws upon, our published works:

www.theschooloflife.com/therapy

THESCHOOLOFLIFE.COM